Samuel! Samuel!

The Story of God's Call to Samuel

We are grateful to the following team of authors for their contributions to *God Loves Me*, a Bible story program for young children. This Bible story, one of a series of fifty-two, was written by Patricia L. Nederveld, managing editor for CRC Publications. Suggestions for using this book were developed by Jesslyn DeBoer, a freelance author from Grand Rapids, Michigan. Yvonne Van Ee, an early childhood educator, served as project consultant and wrote *God Loves Me*, the program guide that accompanies this series of Bible storybooks.

Nederveld has served as a consultant to Title I early childhood programs in Colorado. She has extensive experience as a writer, teacher, and consultant for federally funded preschool, kindergarten, and early childhood programs in Colorado, Texas, Michigan, Florida, Missouri, and Washington, using the *High/Scope* Education Research Foundation curriculum. In addition to writing the *Bible Footprints* church curriculum for four- and five-year-olds, Nederveld edited the revised *Threes* curriculum and the first edition of preschool through second grade materials for the *LiFE* curriculum, all published by CRC Publications.

DeBoer has served as a church preschool leader and as coauthor of the preschool-kindergarten materials for the *LiFE* curriculum published by CRC Publications. She has also written K-6 science and health curriculum for Christian Schools International, Grand Rapids, Michigan, and inspirational gift books for Zondervan Publishing House.

Van Ee is a professor and early childhood program advisor in the Education Department at Calvin College, Grand Rapids, Michigan. She has served as curriculum author and consultant for Christian Schools International and wrote the original *Story Hour* organization manual and curriculum materials for fours and fives.

Photo on page 5: SuperStock; page 20: Rosanne Olson/Tony Stone Images.

Library of Congress Cataloging-in-Publication Data

Nederveld, Patricia L., 1944-
    Samuel! Samuel!: the story of God's call to Samuel /Patricia L. Nederveld.
      p. cm. — (God loves me; bk. 17)
    Summary: Retells the Bible story of God's call to young Samuel, who lived in the temple with Eli the priest. Includes follow-up activities.
    ISBN 1-56212-286-X
    1. Samuel (Biblical figure)—Juvenile literature. 2. Bible stories, English—O.T. Samuel, 1st. 3. Bible games and puzzles. [1. Samuel (Biblical judge) 2. Bible stories—O.T.] I. Title. II. Series: Nederveld, Patricia L., 1944- God loves me; bk. 17.
BS580.S2N35 1998
222'.4309505—dc21

                                    97-32475
                                        CIP
                                        AC

10 9 8 7 6 5 4 3 2 1

Samuel! Samuel!
The Story of God's Call to Samuel

PATRICIA L. NEDERVELD

ILLUSTRATIONS BY LISA WORKMAN

CRC Publications
Grand Rapids, Michigan

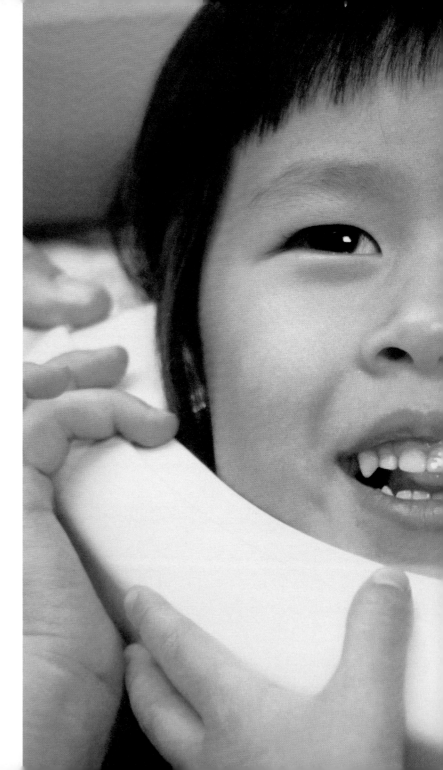

This is a story
from God's
book, the Bible.

It's for <small>say name(s) of
your child(ren).</small>
It's for me too!

1 Samuel 3:1-18

Samuel is a child of God,
he prays to God each day.
He knows that God will hear him,
for God listens when we pray.

Samuel helps Eli the priest.
They work for God each day.
In the temple of the Lord
they live and sleep and pray.

Now Samuel fell asleep one night—
but not for very long!
He woke to someone calling him,
a voice both kind and strong.

"Samuel! Samuel!"

Samuel ran to
find Eli.
"What do
you want?" he
said.
But Eli said, "I
didn't call!
Go back! Go
back to bed!"

Samuel obeyed. He climbed in bed,
but two more times it came.
Someone called to him again—
the voice was just the same!

"Samuel! Samuel!"

" I didn't call you," said Eli. "But here's what you must do. Go back to bed, my little friend, for God is calling you."

"When you hear God's voice again, just answer God this way— 'Speak, Lord. Your child will listen to every word you say!'"

"Samuel!
Samuel!"
God called to him
once more.
And this time he
was ready
to listen to the
Lord!

Samuel grew to
be a man—
he served God
every day.
And best of all,
he listened
to all God had
to say!

wonder if you like to listen to God's words to us in the Bible . . .

Dear God, thank you for your words to us in the Bible. Help us to be good listeners! Amen.

Suggestions for Follow-up

Opening

Greet your little ones by name and tell them you're so glad to *hear* their voices today. Give each child a gentle hug, and invite them to play and learn about a small boy who heard God's voice calling him.

Gather the children around you, and ask them to point to the part of their bodies that helps them hear. Invite the children to play a listening game— "What Do I Hear?" Ahead of time, record sounds that are familiar to your little ones (a baby's cry, barking dog, horn, fire truck siren). Help children identify the sounds on the cassette. Listen for and have children identify sounds inside or outside of your room. Be especially sensitive to a child who may be hearing impaired—show pictures of the sounds you've recorded or bring a "see and say" toy with pictures and sounds. Remind your little ones that we can listen to God when we listen to Bible stories.

Learning Through Play

Learning through play is the best way! The following activity suggestions are meant to help you provide props and experiences that will invite the children to play their way into the Scripture story and its simple truth. Try to provide plenty of time for the children to choose their own activities and to play individually. Use group activities sparingly—little ones learn most comfortably with a minimum of structure.

1. Provide half-sheets of construction paper, 3" x 5" (8 cm x 13 cm) pieces of felt, and cutouts of the figure of Samuel (see Pattern D, Patterns Section, *God Loves Me* program guide). Let children scribble color the cutouts with colors or markers. Show them how to glue the felt mat to the paper and glue the figure to the mat. Use a marker to add a title: "Samuel! Samuel!" To make a puppet picture, sew or glue two felt mats together, leaving one end open to form a sleeping bag, and copy the figures on cardstock. Have the children color the figure, and glue the bag to the paper. Show your little ones how to slip the figure of Samuel in and out of the bag as they help you retell the story.

2. Lay out a Bible or a children's story Bible and Bible storybooks in your play area. Encourage the children to pretend and act out times when families might read the Bible together, such as mealtime or bedtime. Play with them, and read a Bible story together. Praise your little ones for listening to God's word, and remind them that God's word is for everyone—mommies and daddies and children too.

3. Reenact today's story using the simple action rhyme below. As you read or recite the lines, invite the children to imitate your actions.

   Samuel, Samuel went to bed. (lay head on hands)
   "Samuel, Samuel," a voice said. (cup hands around mouth)
   Samuel, Samuel ran to Eli. (jog in place)
   "Samuel, Samuel, it wasn't I." (shake your head, point to self)

Samuel, Samuel heard God say, (point
  upward)
"Samuel, Samuel, listen today." (cup hands by
  ears to listen)

4. Plan time for your little ones to listen to the
sounds around them. You might want to find a
quiet place to sit outside. Have the children
close their eyes and listen for sounds. Help
them identify the sounds of cars, birds, people,
music, airplanes, insects, and so forth. Or try a
listening game inside. Bring a bag full of
noisemakers (whistle, bells, baby rattle or
squeak toy, radio, toy telephone, and so on).
Ask the children to close their eyes tight while
you make noise with each object. No peeking!
When someone guesses, let everyone look to
see if the guess was right. Praise your little ones
for being such good listeners. Be especially
sensitive to a child who may be hearing
impaired. Bring a slate or tablet for the outdoor
exercise, and draw a picture of the object you
hear. Let this child make the noises with the
objects in the bag.

Closing

Sing or say the words from the song "Two Little
Eyes" (Songs Section, *God Loves Me* program
guide) as your little ones follow your actions:

Two little eyes to look to God, (point to each
  eye; point up)
two little ears to hear his Word, (point to
  each ear)
two little feet to walk his ways, (point to
  feet, step in place)
hands to serve God all my days. (put hands
  out, palms up)
  –Words: annonymous

Gather your little ones close around you. Touch
each one and whisper each child's name as you
thank God that the Bible is for each of them.

At Home
Reading to your little one is one of the most
important ways you can help your child learn.
Cuddling close with a book is one way to show
how much you care for and enjoy spending
time with your precious little one. Keep a
basket of Bible storybooks near a favorite
rocker or by your child's bed. Tuck one or two
in a kitchen drawer or your briefcase or
toolbox. Take surprise time-outs to read on a
walk, in the park, on the porch, while waiting
in line. When you read Bible stories together,
your child begins to hear God's words and learn
about God's love. Tell your child to listen extra
carefully because Bible stories are God's way of
talking to us.

Old Testament Stories

Blue and Green and Purple Too! *The Story of God's Colorful World*

It's a Noisy Place! *The Story of the First Creatures*

Adam and Eve *The Story of the First Man and Woman*

Take Good Care of My World! *The Story of Adam and Eve in the Garden*

A Very Sad Day *The Story of Adam and Eve's Disobedience*

A Rainy, Rainy Day *The Story of Noah*

Count the Stars! *The Story of God's Promise to Abraham and Sarah*

A Girl Named Rebekah *The Story of God's Answer to Abraham*

Two Coats for Joseph *The Story of Young Joseph*

Plenty to Eat *The Story of Joseph and His Brothers*

Safe in a Basket *The Story of Baby Moses*

I'll Do It! *The Story of Moses and the Burning Bush*

Safe at Last! *The Story of Moses and the Red Sea*

What Is It? *The Story of Manna in the Desert*

A Tall Wall *The Story of Jericho*

A Baby for Hannah *The Story of an Answered Prayer*

Samuel! Samuel! *The Story of God's Call to Samuel*

Lions and Bears! *The Story of David the Shepherd Boy*

David and the Giant *The Story of David and Goliath*

A Little Jar of Oil *The Story of Elisha and the Widow*

One, Two, Three, Four, Five, Six, Seven! *The Story of Elisha and Naaman*

A Big Fish Story *The Story of Jonah*

Lions, Lions! *The Story of Daniel*

New Testament Stories

Jesus Is Born! *The Story of Christmas*

Good News! *The Story of the Shepherds*

An Amazing Star! *The Story of the Wise Men*

Waiting, Waiting, Waiting! *The Story of Simeon and Anna*

Who Is This Child? *The Story of Jesus in the Temple*

Follow Me! *The Story of Jesus and His Twelve Helpers*

The Greatest Gift *The Story of Jesus and the Woman at the Well*

A Father's Wish *The Story of Jesus and a Little Boy*

Just Believe! *The Story of Jesus and a Little Girl*

Get Up and Walk! *The Story of Jesus and a Man Who Couldn't Walk*

A Little Lunch *The Story of Jesus and a Hungry Crowd*

A Scary Storm *The Story of Jesus and a Stormy Sea*

Thank You, Jesus! *The Story of Jesus and One Thankful Man*

A Wonderful Sight! *The Story of Jesus and a Man Who Couldn't See*

A Better Thing to Do *The Story of Jesus and Mary and Martha*

A Lost Lamb *The Story of the Good Shepherd*

Come to Me! *The Story of Jesus and the Children*

Have a Great Day! *The Story of Jesus and Zacchaeus*

I Love You, Jesus! *The Story of Mary's Gift to Jesus*

Hosanna! *The Story of Palm Sunday*

The Best Day Ever! *The Story of Easter*

Goodbye—for Now *The Story of Jesus' Return to Heaven*

A Prayer for Peter *The Story of Peter in Prison*

Sad Day, Happy Day! *The Story of Peter ad Dorcas*

A New Friend *The Story of Paul's Conversion*

Over the Wall *The Story of Paul's Escape in a Basket*

A Song in the Night *The Story of Paul and Silas in Prison*

A Ride in the Night *The Story of Paul's Escape on Horseback*

The Shipwreck *The Story of Paul's Rescue at Sea*

Holiday Stories

Selected stories from the New Testament to help you celebrate the Christian year

Jesus Is Born! *The Story of Christmas*

Good News! *The Story of the Shepherds*

An Amazing Star! *The Story of the Wise Men*

Hosanna! *The Story of Palm Sunday*

The Best Day Ever! *The Story of Easter*

Goodbye—for Now *The Story of Jesus' Return to Heaven*

These fifty-two books are the heart of *God Loves Me,* a Bible story program designed for young children. Individual books (or the entire set) and the accompanying program guide *God Loves Me* are available from CRC Publications (1-800-333-8300).